# Dolphins

## by Grace Hansen

ABDO
OCEAN LIFE
Kids

**abdopublishing.com**

Published by Abdo Kids, a division of ABDO, PO Box 398166, Minneapolis, Minnesota 55439.

Copyright © 2015 by Abdo Consulting Group, Inc. International copyrights reserved in all countries. No part of this book may be reproduced in any form without written permission from the publisher.

Printed in the United States of America, North Mankato, Minnesota.

102014

012015

 THIS BOOK CONTAINS RECYCLED MATERIALS

Photo Credits: iStock, Shutterstock, Thinkstock

Production Contributors: Teddy Borth, Jennie Forsberg, Grace Hansen

Design Contributors: Laura Rask, Dorothy Toth

Library of Congress Control Number: 2014943714

Cataloging-in-Publication Data

Hansen, Grace.

 Dolphins / Grace Hansen.

  p. cm. -- (Ocean life)

ISBN 978-1-62970-708-2 (lib. bdg.)

Includes index.

1. Dolphins--Juvenile literature.    I. Title.

599.53--dc23

                              2014943714

# Table of Contents

## Dolphins

There are two types of whales. There are baleen and toothed whales. Dolphins are toothed whales.

4

5

Dolphins live in oceans around the world. They like shallow waters. Some species live in rivers.

## Bottlenose Dolphins

Bottlenose dolphins are the most **familiar** species. They grow to be about 8 feet (2.4 m) long.

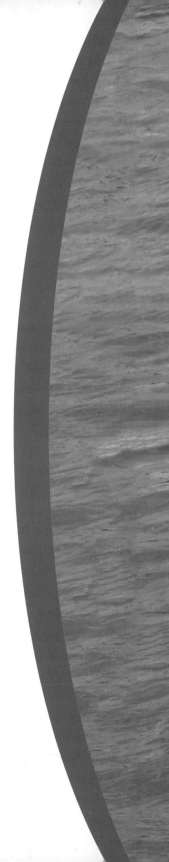

9

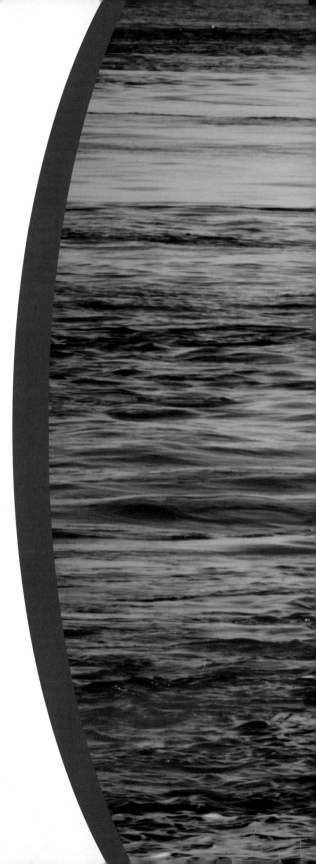

## Orcas

Orcas are the largest dolphins. They are also called killer whales. Orcas can grow to be 25 feet (7.6 m) long.

## Body Parts

Dolphins have five
fins. Dolphins use
fins to move and turn.

3

2

1

4

5

13

Dolphins have a blowhole.

They use this for breathing.

14

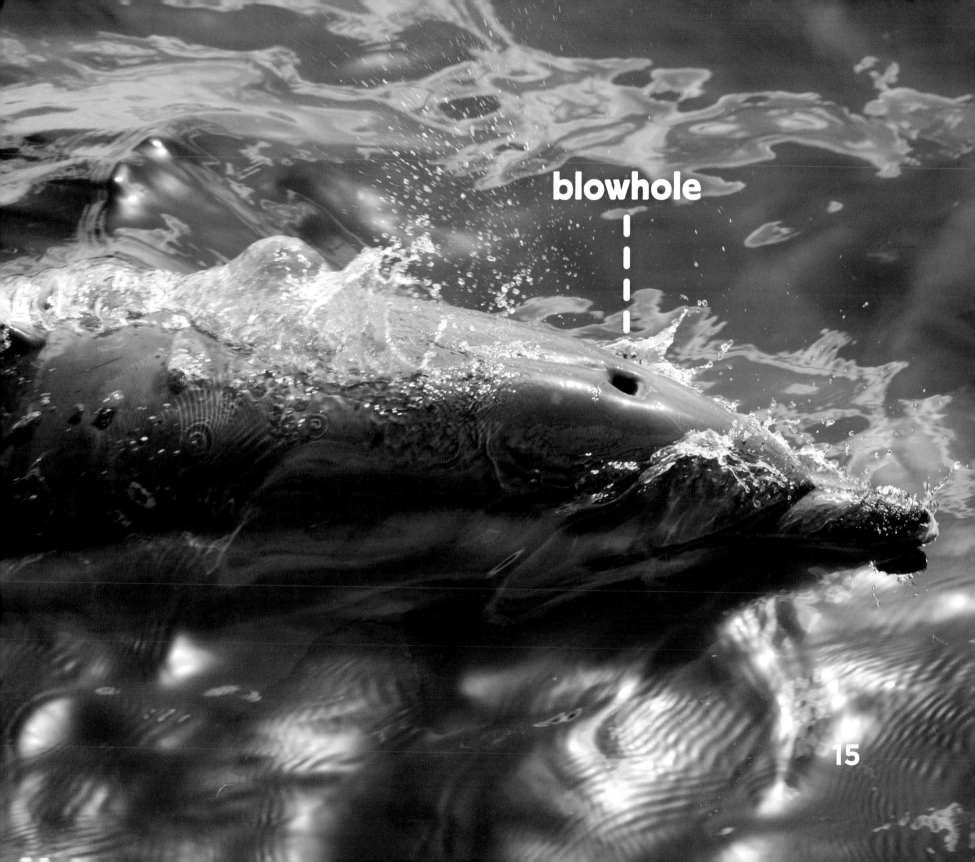

blowhole

15

## Personality

Dolphins are social. They
live in groups called **pods**.
Many members are related.

17

## Baby Dolphins

Baby dolphins are called calves. Females usually have one calf every two to four years. **Twins** are rare.

Calves **nurse** for up to two years. They stay with their mothers for up to eight years.

# More Facts

- There are over 30 species of dolphins. Some live in oceans. Others live in freshwater rivers.

- Every dolphin has a unique **dorsal fin**.

- Most dolphins can live for a very long time. Bottlenose dolphins can live for over 40 years. Orcas can live up to 80 years.

# Glossary

**dorsal fin** – a fin that is found on a dolphin's back.

**familiar** – well known or recognizable.

**nurse** – feed young milk that is made by the mother.

**pod** – a group of dolphins (up to around 12) that stay together to hunt and protect each other.

**twins** – two animals born at the same time from the same mother.

# Index

## abdokids.com

Use this code to log on to abdokids.com and access crafts, games, videos, and more!

Abdo Kids Code:
**ODK7082**